Arduino

The ultimate Arduino guide for beginners, including Arduino programming, Arduino cookbook, tips, tricks, and more!

Table of Contents

Introduction 1

Chapter 1: The Basics of the Arduino Platform 2

Chapter 2: Getting Started with Arduino... 9

Chapter 3: Dictionary of Words to Know with Arduino...................... 13

Chapter 4: Testing Out Arduino and Learning Your First Code 16

Chapter 5: Coding for Arduino... 24

Chapter 6: Some Other Projects You Can Work On with Arduino 40

Conclusion.. 54

Introduction

Thank you for taking the time to pick up this guide book all about Arduino.

This book covers the topic of the Arduino microcomputer, and will teach you all about how to use and program your own for a variety of projects!

In the following chapters, you will discover how the Arduino works and how to write code for the Arduino. You will also learn about the syntax used on the Arduino system, and even how how to create your very own Arduino projects!

At the completion of this book you will have a good base understanding of Arduino, and be ready to create some basic Arduino projects of your very own!

Once again, thanks for choosing this book, I hope you find it to be helpful!

Chapter 1: The Basics of the Arduino Platform

Before we get too far into this guidebook, we need to first get acquainted with Arduino and what it's all about. Arduino is basically a microcontroller and software that is open sourced, programmable, and based on using the ATMega chip. Although it is designed as a type of prototyping platform, it is usable on a variety of electronics projects, whether it is being used as a temporary addition or it is embedded into the project.

The Arduino board can also be programmed using the Arduino software, which is easy and fun to use, even if you are a beginner. If you have used the Java or the C/C++ programming languages, you will find that they are pretty similar to what you will be using with the Arduino programming language. The idea behind this programming language is that it's meant to be simple yet powerful, so that beginners as well as those with more experience with programming will be able to benefit equally from this platform.

Since Arduino is considered an open source platform, you are able to access the source code as well as the schematics to it without issue. It is open for anyone to use, to make changes to, develop, and to use as they see fit, so you are able to delve in as far as you would like with the code. Some beginners may be more interested in just using some of the premade code to start their projects, while those who are a bit more experienced may be interested in creating their own Arduino boards. Thanks to its popularity, there are many communities devoted to this language, which makes it simple to ask questions, find information, watch tutorials, and get help with coding when needed.

The platform of Arduino is quite basic, comes with two main components, namely:

- The software - this is going to be the Integrated Development Environment (IDE) that will run on the computer. It is used for uploading and writing the programming codes that you want to go onto the physical board, so that the project will do what you want.

- The hardware - this is the circuit board or the microcontroller that can be physically programmable. There are a few different types of Arduino boards that you are able to use depending on the project at hand.

Both of these parts come together to make your project work. The hardware or Arduino board is the part that is going to respond to what you are sending through with the software, and it will often be used in your projects to make things blink up, move, or perform some other kind of action.

With that being said, you are also going to need to make sure that the software is in place. The IDE is free when you are using the Arduino programming language so it is really easy to get set up on your computer. The IDE works well with any of the operating systems that you may have on your computer, whether you are working with Windows, Linux, or Mac OSX. One thing to keep in mind is that if you are using Windows 7 or earlier for your operating system, you are going to have to take a few extra steps in order to get the drive to work with your Arduino board, and we will cover those steps shortly.

If you are a beginner with programming and electronics, you will find that the Arduino platform is pretty easy to learn how to use. At the same time, it provides the power that an advanced programmer or electronics enthusiast needs for more complicated projects.

What am I able to do with Arduino?

There are a lot of different programming languages that you are able to choose from, and a lot of Arduino alternatives. This begs the question; "why choose Arduino?"

The answer to this question is the large number of different possibilities that Arduino provides. There are thousands of projects all throughout the world that have used the Arduino platform for their creation, and these range from the most basic functions, to advanced programs and robotics. For example, the Arduino platform has been used to create and power the following:

- Home automation systems

- Custom keyboards and mouse

- Musical instruments

- Clocks

- Advertising displays

- The 'like' counters on Facebook

- Human and computer interfaces

- Cocktail makers

- MIDI controllers

- In-car computers

- Art installations

- Robots

That is just a partial list of what you are able to do with the Arduino platform. The main features that you can enjoy from the Arduino board include its ability to read data from sensors, send and receive digital signals, and connect via a serial to a computer. In your Arduino projects you'll be able to control multiple things, including relays, motors, LCDs, and LEDs. You will also be able to read out values from sensors, such as the piezos, light dependent resistors, and the potentiometers.

The digital pins that you are able to use with the Arduino will allow you to write or read 5V values. You will then be able to use a pin in order to turn on the LED, with the resistor. It is then possible to send a signal to the relay if you would like to operate at a higher voltage with some types of appliances, such as house lights and televisions. You can also send messages for when you want to turn on and off the motors, and you can even check to see when a button has been pressed. That all may sound advanced right now, but basically if there is something that can be controlled with the help of a current, you'll be able to integrate and control it in an Arduino project.

The analog pins that you will use will give you the ability to read the voltage that comes in between the 0v and the 5v. this can help you to read from the Arduino sensors. Since there are a variety of sensors you can use, this allows you to control a variety of projects with the Arduino.

Most people who hear about this process assume that they are simply going to be able to use the program in order to control basic electronic circuits. However, there are a few other pieces of technology that you should consider using the Arduino with as well. For example, it is possible to use this programming language to send data back to a computer, allowing you to control software such as Max/MSP and Processing. You can also send this data over a USB with most of the Arduino board models that you make. Some models will also work with Ethernet or Bluetooth ports so that you can continue the communication even without a Wi-Fi connection.

For those who are interested in electronic products and robotics, the Arduino programming language is one of the best to get started with. It is quite simple to use, and works with the C++ programming language. This results in a wide range of versatility, combined with adequate power to create and run a broad variety of projects. In addition, there is a big library of free code compiled by other users, making it simple for beginners to get started.

If you are interested in programming, electronics, or robotics, the Arduino programming language is a perfect choice. As you will soon discover, it is relatively simple to learn and it has all the features and power that you might need.

What am I not able to do with Arduino?

So we've covered that there are a lot of different uses for the Arduino, but where do its limitations lie? There are a few downsides to the Arduino that may mean it's not the right choice for you. For example, Arduino isn't known for having a lot of processing power, so any really intensive task is not going to be possible. This means that you aren't going to be able to use the language in order to process, record, or even output audio and video, though you can use it to output graphics to LCD or TFT screens.

While some people may feel that this language and the boards that come with it should work like a regular computer, this just isn't so. You will not be able to hook up a keyboard or a webcam to the system, and it does not have an operating system like you may find with some Arduino alternatives, such as the Raspberry Pi.

Overall though the Arduino is a fantastic piece of technology, which will meet the needs of most programmers and electronics enthusiasts.

Who can use Arduino?

One of the nice things about Arduino is that anyone is able to use it. Experts like to use it because there is a lot of variety to what they can do, and it is easier than ever to make changes to their work. On the flip side, even if you have never worked with programming or electronics, you will be able to get started and have your first project running in no time. This first project may be something basic such as making the LED flash on and off in a pattern of your choosing, but it's a start, and won't take you long!

The benefits of choosing Arduino

If you're still not sure if the Arduino is the best choice for you, here are a few of its benefits as compared to other alternative technologies.

- Able to work across platforms - the IDE for Arduino is able to work on many different operating systems including Linux, Mac OSX, and Windows. This is beneficial, especially since most other microcontrollers on the market will only work with Windows.

- Simple environment - the IDE is really easy to use when it comes to Arduino. It is a lot like C++ but is even simpler to use. This is great for beginners who want to get into programming and electronics but are intimidating by the potential learning curve.

- Extensible hardware and open source - the board plans for Arduino are published as open source. This means that anyone is able to use them and make changes to them when needed. This is nice for circuit designers because they are able to create new and improved versions whenever they desire.

- Open source software - in addition to the board plans being open sourced, the software is too. The IDE is published with tools that are open source, so that programmers with experience are able to expand on it thanks to the C++ libraries. You can also use the AVR-C code with Arduino, or even add these directly into your code.

- Free to use - unlike some of the other programming languages that you can choose from, this is one that is free to use. While you will need to go out and purchase the board that you would like to use based on the project you are working on, the software that you need as well as everything else that is needed to start your project is free to use. This makes it easier than ever to experiment with your projects, helping you to learn the process without worrying about the costs associated.

- A big community - when you are learning how to program for Arduino, or learning any new programming language for that matter, it is always beneficial to have a big community available to answer your questions. Arduino has a great community that will be able to answer any questions, provide you with tutorials, and so much more. This really is one of the best components of Arduino!

As you can see, there is just so much to love about Arduino! Now that you have a good understanding of the Arduino system, its pros and cons, and how it works, it's time to begin learning how to use your Arduino for a variety of projects. We start this off in the next chapter where we will take a look at the different Arduino boards, and how to get started with using the software!

Chapter 2: Getting Started with Arduino

Since this is a platform that is widely popular and is constantly expanding and changing, it is important to keep in mind that you will have to continue learning about the programming language as changes to it occur. To begin with though, we are going to spend some time learning the basics that you will need to know to get started with Arduino. To begin, there are two essentials that you will need; the software to make this work, and the Arduino board.

Understanding the Arduino board

Before you go out and purchase an Arduino board, you will need to understand some of the basic features of these boards and their uses. There are a few types of boards that are available, and each of them have different capabilities and benefits. While they will differ in terms of what they are able to do and how they look, most of the boards you come across will have the following components in common:

- Barrel Jack and USB - all the boards will have some method for you to connect them to a power source. Most of them will come with a USB connection so that you can upload your codes onto them. You can also choose to connect them with a barrel jack which will essentially let you plug the board into the wall.

- Pins - the pins are where you are going to construct your circuits by connecting in the wires. There are a few types of pins that you can use on the boards and they are each used for a specific function. Some of the most common pins that you will find include:

  - GND: this is short for Gourd. They are the pins that you will use in order to ground your circuit.

  - 5v and 3.3V: these are the pins that will supply either 5 volts or 3.3 Volts of power.

- Analog: these are the pins that will be seen under the 'Analog In' label. These are the ones that you can use for reading signals from the analog sensors, and then these signals are going to be converted into a digital value.

- Digital: these are going to be across from the analog pins and will be under the 'Digital' label. These are the pins that are used for the input and output of the digital signal.

- PWM: in many of the Arduino boards, there will be a (PWM~) label that is next to the Digital one. This basically means that the pins are able to be used as either normal digital pins, or for a signal that is called Pulse-Width Modulation.

- AREF: this is short form for Analog Reference. This is the pin that you can use to set the upper limit of the external voltage for the analog pins, usually between 0 and 5 volts, though it is often left alone.

- Reset button - this button should be there to allow the pin to rest to the ground, and to restart the code that is already loaded on the board. It is a good way to test out code a few times. It will not reset everything to a clean state, and won't fix any problems that exist in your code.

- Power LED Indicator - this should be a tiny LED light that should have the word "ON" right next to it. It is going to light up when you plug your board into a power source.

- Transmit and Receive LEDs - these are in place to give an indication that the board is either receiving or transmitting data. This is useful when you are trying to load up a new program to the board and you want to see if it is being received.

- Main Integrated Circuit (IC) - this is a little black piece that has metal legs that will attach to the board. Think of it as the brains of the board. The IC will differ between boards, but most are from the ATMEL company. Make sure to know which kind of IC you are using before loading up a new program though because this sometimes does make a difference.

- Voltage regulator - this is the component of the board that is going to control how much voltage is able to get onto the board. It has the ability to turn away any extra voltage that is trying to get into the board. It is not able to handle anything that is more than 20 Volts though, so make sure to not use a power supply higher than this or it will destroy the board.

In addition to picking the right board for your project, you need to consider the other hardware that you may want to add on. The board can do a lot of stuff on its own, but it gets a lot of the power you are looking for when you add on some additional hardware. For the basics that we will be learning, it is not such a big deal, but as you progress you may want to consider adding on additional components to get a bit more power.

Getting the software hooked up

After you have had some time to go through and pick out the hardware that you would like to use, including the board you want for the project, it is time to install the IDE for Arduino. This is basically the environment, or the software, that you will need in order to write out the code for the microcontroller and to attach all the circuit components. Without the IDE in place, you would not be able to write out the code and the microcontroller and board would have no idea what you want them to do.

To start, you simply need to visit the Arduino website at www.arduino.cc in order to download the IDE. The IDE will download as a receive a zip folder. Open this up and then save it in a location on your computer that is easy for you to remember.

Once that's done, you will need to run the Arduino.EXE file so that the installation can get started. You simply need to follow the command prompts that come up in order to get everything installed. Once the IDE is set up and you have all the right hardware components, you are ready to move onto the next step of using this programming language!

Chapter 3: Dictionary of Words to Know with Arduino

If you are new to Arduino, it is a good idea to learn some of the lingo so that you are able to read out instructions and understand what we're talking about in the next few chapters.

The most common words that you need to know are as follows:

- **C++** - this is a programming language, the one that you will most likely use when working in the Arduino IDE. If you don't already know how to use this language, don't worry. You will easily pick up the basics as you tackle a few Arduino projects.

- **CPU** - this stands for Central Processing Unit and it is often known as the processor. It is basically the electronic circuitry that is inside of the computer, and it is in charge of carrying out all the instructions for the computer.

- **Driver** - this is a software that is going to allow a computer to connect and then communicate with a device or the hardware. Without using the right driver, the hardware you will try to connect to a computer won't be able to work properly. Depending on the type of operating system you choose to work with, you may need to install a new driver in order to read the Arduino board.

- **Environment** - when it comes to computing jargon, the environment is going to be the specific configuration of a hardware platform, as well as the operating system that it is going to run on.

- **Ground** - in electrical engineering, this is going to be the reference point in the circuit where the voltages are measured, or else the common wiring point.

- **I/O** - this is short for input/output, which is going to describe a device, operation, or program that is able to

13

transfer data to or from a computer so that it can interact with the outside world. For example, if you push a button, that is the input, a light bulb will turn on, which is the output.

- **LED** - this is an acronym that stands for Light Emitting Diode, and it is a two lead semiconductor light source. The LEDs are advantageous compared to other light sources because they are smaller, have a longer lifespan, and they don't take up as much energy.

- **Microcontroller** - this is a computer that is present inside a single integrated circuit that will be programmed in order to perform specific tasks. These are basically the brains behind automatically controlled electronic devices, whether you are talking about things like robots, microwaves, washing machines, cameras, and even cell phones.

- **Open source** - a program that has an open source code means that its code is going to be made freely available to the public to modify or use. The developers are able to share the products with the public who will then be able to improve it, redistribute it, and modify it as they wish.

- **Sketch** - this is the term that is used to describe an Arduino program. A chunk of code will be written in order to command the board to work in a specific way, and this is code known as the 'sketch'.

- **Shield** - this is a circuit board that you are able to place on top of the Arduino for a variety of reasons. They are basically called this because of how they fit over the Arduino board like a shield.

- **IDE** - this one stands for Integrated Development Environment, and it is the software application that will run in order to provide you with the tools that are needed to program the Arduino boards. It will include a debugger, build automation, and a source code editor.

With Arduino, it is open source so you are able to download it online and use it as much as you want to make changes to code, or write code from scratch.

- **PWM (Pulse Width Modulation** - this is a term that is used to describe a type of digital signal that can be used for a variety of purposes. For the most part, it is used to control how much power is going to be supplied to the electrical devices.

- **Voltage** - this is the amount of energy that occurs between two points of a circuit, and it is going to be measured with the standard unit of V for Volt.

Having an understanding of these terms can make working with Arduino a lot easier. Try and learn these words before we move onto writing code in the next chapter.

Chapter 4: Testing Out Arduino and Learning Your First Code

Now that you have an understanding of the Arduino system and how to set it all up, it's time to get right into programming and writing code. This may seem a little bit intimidating if you're new to programming, but the basics are quite simple and intuitive with Arduino.

Getting started on your first few projects does not have to be difficult. You will find that as long as the IDE is in place, you learn the right code, and your computer is able to recognize the hardware or the board that you are using, it is pretty easy to complete some of the basic projects.

The code is also quite easy to understand and learn. If you have done any programming in the past, especially if you have worked with C++ programming language in particular, you will find that it is going to use the same kinds of coding and structures as you are used to. If you haven't done much with coding or haven't worked with the C++ programming yet, you should be able to get the hang of it quickly by looking at the examples in this book.

By this point, you should already have the Arduino IDE set up along with the hardware that you need. Now it is time to get a bit of testing in with the Arduino system, both to make sure that it is working properly and that as a beginner, you are getting a feel for how the system works. Next, we will work on your first code which is learning how to activate an LED light on the board. For this example, we are going to use the Arduino UNO (R3) board, but you can also make a few small modifications to make this project work on any board that you choose.

To get started with this first project, there are four tools that you are going to need:

- A computer. The computer needs to be relatively new and have either a Windows operating system with XP or above, or Linux or Mac operating systems. Make sure that the IDE for Arduino is installed.

- A microcontroller for Arduino. This is the circuit board we talked about earlier in the book.

- A USB A-to-B cable so that you are able to connect the board that you chose to the computer.

- An LED

With these items, you are ready to get started with your first Arduino project!

Plugging in the board

For the most part, the Arduino boards are going to be powered by a USB connection into a computer, or an external power supply, such as plugging it into the wall with a barrel jack. It is necessary to plug the board into the computer if you would like to have it work with the Arduino IDE. Once you have uploaded all the programming from the IDE over to the circuit board, you will not need to plug it into the computer, and you can choose to use a wall power supply if you want.

So for this part, you will need to bring out the USB cable and connect the Arduino board with the computer. The moment that these two are connected, you should notice that the LED light that is labeled "ON" will start to blink pretty quickly. This is going to happen because it is the default program that is already created and stored on the chip for the board. With this project, we are going to override this default program and make it so that the LED is going to blink on and off at a slower pace, with about two seconds in between each blink, rather than the fast pace it is currently operating at.

As mentioned before, there are a number of different types of boards that you are able to use to make your own projects, and each of them may plug in a slightly different way. You need to make sure that the one that you pick out is able to plug into the computer. Remember that it has to be able to plug into the computer if you would like to get the code to upload to the board. If it is only able to plug into the wall rather than the computer, you are going to find that it is almost impossible to use the code that you want.

Install the drivers

The next step is to install the drivers. If you are using a Windows XP, Windows Vista, or a Windows 7 computer, you will need to go through this process the first time that you use a new Arduino board. If you are using Windows 8 and higher or any of the other operating systems, you will be able to skip over these steps. To install the drivers, you will need to follow the proceeding steps:

- After the board is plugged in, the Windows operating system is going to start with the driver installation process. You will notice however that the process is going to fail after a few minutes.

- You can then go to the Start Menu and then click on the Control Panel

- Navigate through the Control Panel until you get to System and Security. Click on the System tab.

- Once this window is up, you can click to open up Device Manager

- Look under Ports. Here you are going to see an open port that is called Arduino UNO (COMxx). However, if the

Ports section doesn't show up, you can look under the tab for Other Devices and do a search for Unknown Device.

- Next, you can Right click on this and then choose the option for Update Driver Software.

- Select the Browse my computer for driver software option

- Finally, you will be able to find and select the file that is called Arduino.inf, which you are going to be able to find in the Drivers folder of the Arduino Software download. If you are going with an IDE that is an older version, you will need to go with the file that is called Arduino UNO.inf.

- From this point, the Windows operating system will be able to finish up the installation on its own.

Keep in mind that you are only going to have to do these steps if you have an older version of Windows operating system. If you have Windows 8 or newer, or any of the other operating systems, they are not going to have issues with uploading the IDE and the other information that you need, so these steps are not necessary.

For the other operating systems that you are going to use, you will be able to just plug in the parts that you need and you are set. You will see that they are going to recognize the drive automatically, and be ready to use straight away.

Working on the launch and sketch

Once the IDE is installed, it is now time to do a test drive of the board with the first program. This is a good place to learn how to use the programming language if you aren't familiar with it, as well as make sure that the IDE and the board are working the way that you want.

Before we start writing code, there are a few things to be aware of. As mentioned earlier, the codes are often called sketches in this language and you are going to be writing them in C++. If you aren't familiar with C++, don't worry, we will be starting slowly and you'll get the hang of the basics in no time.

Every sketch that you are doing will need to have two void type functions that will not return a value; these are the loop() and the setup() functions. The setup() method is going to be run just once, right after the Arduino board is powered up and going, and the loop() method is going to keep on running until you unplug the board. The setup() part is where you will want to perform the initialization steps, and the loop() is basically going to be the code that you want to run continuously over and over again.

So a good example of a basic code in this language would be:

void setup(){

   }

void loop(){

}

Of course this is pretty basic and if you typed this into the IDE, you would have nothing happening. You will need to add in a few more parts to the code to get it to do what you want, but this is a good way to see how the code is going to be laid out.

So now, let's get started and work on our first program with the following steps:

1. Make sure that the board is plugged in and that the application for Arduino is launched.

2. Open up the Blink example sketch. To find this sketch, you will just need to go to File > Examples > 1.Basics > Blink

3. You can then select the type of Arduino board that you will be using for this. To do this just click on Tools > Board > your board type.

4. Now you are able to choose the serial or COM port that the Arduino is attached to. You can do this by clicking on Tools > Port > COMxx.

If you do not know which serial device is with your board, you will have to look at all the available ports to locate this information. If it is still confusing, you can unplug the board while watching the computer. The port that disappears when you unplug the board is the one that the board is using, and it is the one that you should pick.

Upload and make the light blink

Make sure that for this step you have the board still connected to the computer and that the Blink sketch is open. Now you can press on the Upload button. You will need to wait for a few seconds, but then you should be able to see that the LEDs for the RX and TX are going to be flashing while the program uploads to the board. If this upload is successful, you are going to see a message that says 'Done Uploading' on the status bar of your Blink Sketch.

If you did this whole process correctly, the orange LED light for "ON" should be blinking slowly, rather than in the fast manner that it was earlier. Congrats! You have just completed programming your first thing with the Arduino board!

I followed the steps and it didn't work!

If you went through all the steps we discussed above and the light is still blinking fast rather than slowing down, there may be a few issues that are causing you some difficulties. Some of the things that you can try to do if the program didn't work are:

- Make sure that you selected the right type of board. If you are using a different type of board than the one you selected, the program won't work. If you selected the wrong board, you can start again by clicking on the correct one under Tools > Board.

- Next, check that the right port is selected with the Tools > Serial port menu. If the wrong port is selected, this could be the issue.

- You can also check and see if the drivers for the board you are using are installed properly. You can go into the Tools > Serial Port part inside the Arduino IDE with the board still connected. You should notice that there is an extra item in the IDE that wasn't there before you plugged in the board.

Checking these should ensure that the program worked, and the light should now be flashing slower than before!

Light an LED

Now that you have activated the Arduino, it is time to move onto our second project. This project is a good one for beginners who are new to circuitry. For this one to work, you will simply need the Arduino board, as well as an LED. When you are ready, follow these simple steps:

1. Plug in the Arduino board.

2. Open up another example of a sketch. To do this click on File > Examples > Basics > BareMinimum. This is going to open up a new window that has a simple sketch. This is going to be like the framework for the program you want to work on.

3. You can connect the LEDs anode, the pin that is longer, to pin 13 on the board, and then the shorter pin, or the cathode, to the adjacent GND pin.

4. Go to the setup() part of the sketch and add in the code *pinMode(13, OUTPUT);*. This command will run once, so that the board is configured and that it is ready to run your program.

5. You will then work on the loop() section. Under here you will write out *digitalWrite(13, HIGH);*. This is going to set it up so that pin 13 is the output pin that will have the high voltage level.

When it is all done the sketch that you should have will be:

void setup(){

pinModel(13, OUTPUT):

}

void loop(){

digitalWrite(13, HIGH):

}

When this is all completed, you will be able to hit on the Upload button and wait a few moments until the 'Done Uploading' message shows up in the status bar of your IDE. Now, look over at the board and see if the LED lights up. If so, you went through and completed this process correctly!

Chapter 5: Coding for Arduino

Coding for the Arduino means learning a new language, but fortunately, it's not nearly as complex as that may sound. In the same way that mathematics has its own set of symbols to denote various functions like addition, subtraction, and multiplication, there are different symbols and terms used when coding for Arduino. Below is a list of the terms and words that are used in Arduino IDE coding and how to use them.

Structure

setup()

This is the function called on when the sketch starts, and will run only once after startup or reset. You can use it to start variables, pin modes, or the use of libraries (specific terms you can download for extra functionality).

loop()

The loop function requires the Arduino microcontroller board to repeat a function multiple times, continuously or until a certain variable or condition is met. You will set the condition for it to stop the loop or you will have it loop continuously until you detach the Arduino from the power source or turn it off.

CONTROL STRUCTURES

If

This that links a condition or input to an output. It means that *if* a certain condition has been met, a specific output or response of the microcontroller will occur. For example, *if* the thermometer to which the microcontroller is attached measures more than 75 degrees Fahrenheit, you might write the code to then direct the Arduino to send a signal to your air conditioning unit to turn on to decrease the temperature back to 75 degrees.

24

If...Else

This is like the *If* conditional but it specifies another action that the microcontroller will take if the condition for the first action is not met. This gives you an option of performing two different actions in two different circumstances with one piece of code.

While

This is a loop that will continue indefinitely until the expression to which it is connected becomes false. That is, it would perform a certain function until a parameter is met and the statement that is set as the condition is made false.

Do... While

This is like the *while* statement but it always runs at least once because it tests the variable at the end of the function rather than at the beginning.

Break

This is an emergency exit of sorts from a function of the microcontroller. It is used to exit a *do, for,* or *while* loop without meeting the condition that must be met to exit that part of the functionality.

Continue

This is like a *break* in a *loop* or *do, for,* or *while* in that it skips the rest of the iteration of the loop. However, it only does so temporarily until it checks on the condition of the loop, at which point it proceeds with any required additional iterations of the loop.

Return

This is the way to stop a function, and it returns a value with which the function terminated to the calling function, or the function that is asking for the information.

Goto

This piece of code tells the microcontroller to move to another place, not consecutive, in the coded program. It transfers the flow to another place in the program. Its use is generally discouraged by C language programmers, but it can definitely simplify a program.

SYNTAX

; (semicolon)

This is used like a period in the English language: it ends a statement. If you want to be sure that a statement is closed, used the semicolon at the end. Be sure, however, that the statement closed by the semicolon is complete, or else your code will not function properly.

{} (curly braces)

These have many complex functions, but the thing you must know is that when you insert a beginning curly brace, you *must* follow it with an ending curly brace. This is called keeping the braces balanced, and is vital to getting your program working.

// (single-line comment)

If you would like to remind yourself or tell others something about how your code functions, use this code to begin the comment, and make sure that it only takes up one line. This will not transfer to the processor of the microcontroller but rather will live in the code and be a reference to you and anyone who is reading the code manually.

/* */ (multi-line comment)

This type of comment is opened by the /* and it spans more than one line. It can itself contain a single line comment but cannot contain another multi-line comment. Be sure to close the comment with */ or else the rest of your code will be considered a comment and not implemented.

#define

This defines a certain variable as a constant value. It gives a name to that value as a sort of shorthand for that value. These do not take up any memory space on the chip so they can be useful in conserving space. Once the code is compiled, or taken together as a program, the compiler will replace any instance of the constant as the value that is used to define it.

NOTE: This statement does NOT use a semicolon at the end. Do not put a semicolon at the end or you will receive error messages and the program will not function.

#include

This is used to include other libraries in your sketch, that is, to include other words and coding language in your sketch that would not otherwise be included. For example, you could include AVR C libraries or many tools, or pieces of code, from the various C libraries.

NOTE: Do NOT add the semicolon at the end of this statement, just as you would exclude it from the #define statement. If you do include a semicolon to close the statement, you will receive error messages and the program will not work.

ARITHMETIC OPERATORS

= (assignment operator)

This assigns a value to a variable and replaces the variable with the assigned value throughout the operation in which it appears. This is different than == which evaluates whether two variables or a variable and a set value are equal. The double equal signs function more like the single equal sign in mathematics and algebra than the single equal sign in the Arduino IDE.

+ (addition)

This does what you might expect it would do: it adds two values, or the value to a variable, or two to a fixed constant. One thing that you must take into account is that there is a maximum for variable values in the C programming languages. This means that, if your variable maxes out at 32,767, then adding 1 to the variable will give you a negative result, -32,768. If you expect that the values will be greater than the absolute maximum value allowable, you can still perform the operations, but you will have to instruct the microcontroller what to do in the case of negative results. In addition, as well as in subtraction, multiplication, and division, you place the resulting variable on the left and the operation to the right of the = or ==.

Also, another thing to keep in mind is that whatever type of data you input into the operation will determine the type of data that is output by the operation. We will look at types of data later, but for example, if you input integers, which are whole numbers, you will receive an answer rounded to the nearest whole number.

- (subtraction)

This operation, like the addition sign, does what you would expect: it subtracts two values from each other, whether they both are variables or one is a constant value. Again, you will have to watch out for values greater than the maximum integer value. Remember to place the resulting variable on the left of the equal sign or signs, and the operation on the right.

* (multiplication)

With multiplication especially, you will need to be careful to define what happens if the value you receive from the operation is greater than the greatest allowable value of a piece of data. This is because multiplication especially grows numbers to large, large values.

/ (division)

Remember to place the resulting variable on the left of the operation, and the values that you are dividing on the right side of the operation.

% (modulo)

This operation gives you the remainder when an integer is divided by another integer. For example, if you did $y = 7 \% 5$, the result for y would be 2, since 5 goes into seven once and leaves a remainder of 2. Remember, you must use integer values for this type of operation.

Comparison Operators

== (equal to)

This operator checks to see if the data on the left side of the double equal signs matches the data on the right side, that is, whether they are equal. For example, you might ask the pin attached to the temperature gauge $t == 75$, and if the temperature is exactly 75 degrees, then the microcontroller will perform a certain task, whether it be turning off the heating or cooling, or turning off a fan.

29

!= (not equal to)

This is the mirror image of the previous operation. You could just as easily write a program to test *t != 75* and set up the microcontroller to turn on a heating lamp, turn on a fan, or ignite the wood in the fireplace if this statement is true. Between == and !=, you can cover all the possible conditions that input might give your microcontroller.

< (less than)

This is a simple operation that mirrors what it does in mathematics and algebra: it tests whether a value is less than another value. If this statement is true, then you can program a certain response from your microcontroller, or, in other words, program an output for such input.

> (greater than)

This operation test is one value on the left is greater than the value on the right. If the value on the left is equal to or less than the value on the right, the statement becomes false. Only in cases where the value on the left is greater than the value on the right will your true statement response of the microcontroller be triggered.

<= (less than or equal to)

This is a similar comparison operator to the less than operator, but it becomes a false statement *only* when the value to the left is greater than the value on the right. This means that <= is the absolute opposite of >. For example, if $x <= y$ is true, then $x > y$ is necessarily false.

>= *(greater than or equal to)*

The greater than or equal to statement only becomes false if the value on the left is less than the value on the right. Greater than or equal to has an absolute opposite as well, the less than. *If a >= b is true, whether a is greater than b or a is equal to b, then a < b is necessarily false.*

Variables

CONSTANTS

HIGH

This value is different based on whether the pin is set up as an input or an output. Should the pin be an input, it will read HIGH if:

    1) A voltage greater than 3.0V is present on a 5V board

    OR

    2) A voltage greater than 2.0V is present on a 3.3V board.

If the pin is set up as an output, it will output as follows:

    1) It will output 5V from a 5V board

    OR

    2) It will output 3.3V from a 3.3V board.

LOW

This value is different based on whether the pin is set up as an input or and output. Should the pin be an input, it will read LOW if:

1) A voltage less than 1.5V is present on a 5V board

   OR

2) A voltage greater than 1.0V is present on a 3.3V board.

If the pin is set up as an output, it will output as follows:

1) It will output 0V from a 5V board

AND, similarly,

2) It will output 0V from a 3.3V board.

INPUT

In the input state, a digital pin will require very little of the processing power and energy from the microcontroller and battery. Instead, it is simply measuring and indicating to the microcontroller its measurements. The rest of the work is done by the microcontroller and the output pins.

OUTPUT

These are very good at powering LED's because they are in a low-impedance state, meaning they let energy flow freely through them without much resistance. Output pins take their directions from the microcontroller once it has processed the information given by the input pins, and the output pins power whatever mechanism will perform the intended task.

INPUT_PULLUP

This is what mode you will want to use when connected to a button or a switch. There is a lot of resistance involved in the INPUT_PULLUP state. This means that it is best used for Boolean-like situations, such as a switch either being on or off.

When there are only two states and not much in between, use INPUT_PULLUP.

LED_BUILTTIN

This code references and calls on the built-in LED. It is useful for debugging your work. The built-in LED is connected to pin 13 on most boards.

true

In a Boolean sense, any integer that is not zero is true. 1 is true, 200 is true, -3 is true, etc. This would be the case when a statement matches reality. One of your pins might be testing a value, and the statement is it trying to match is $y \mathrel{!}= 35$, so if the pin receives information that the value of y is 25, then the statement $25 \mathrel{!}= 35$ is true.

false

This is part of a Boolean Constant, meaning that a statement is false, or that its logic does not match reality. For example, you could have a statement, $x > 7$ and the value the microcontroller receives for x is 3. This would make the statement *false*. It would then be defined as 0 (zero).

integer constants

These are constants that are used by the sketch directly and are in base 10 form, or integer form. You can change the form that the integer constants are written in by preceding the integer with a special notation signifying binary notation (base 2), octal notation (base 8), or hexadecimal notation (base 16), for example.

floating point constants

These save space in the program by creating a shorthand for a long number in scientific notation. Each time the floating point constant appears, it is evaluated at the value that you dictate in your code.

DATA TYPES

Void

This is used in a function declaration to tell the microcontroller that no information is expected to be returned with this function. For example, you would use it with the *setup()* or *loop()* functions.

Boolean

Boolean data holds one of two values: true or false. This could be true of any of the arithmetic operator functions or of other functions. You will use *&&* if you want two conditions to be true simultaneously for the Boolean to be true, *||* if you want one of two conditions to be met, either one setting off the output response, and *!* for not true, meaning that if the operator is *not* true, then the Boolean is true.

Char

This is a character, such as a letter. It also has a numeric value, such that you can perform arithmetic functions on letters and characters. If you want to use characters literally, you will use a single quote for a single character, *'A'* and a double quote for multiple characters, *"ABC"* such that all characters are enclosed in quotes. This means the microcontroller will output these characters verbatim if the given conditions are met. The numbers -128 to 127 are used to signify various signed characters.

Unsigned Char

This is the same as a character but uses the numbers 0 to 255 to signify characters instead of the "signed" characters which include negatives. This is the same as the byte data type.

Byte

This type of data stores a number from 0 to 255 in an 8-bit system of binary numbers. For example, B10010 is the number 18, because this uses a base 2 system.

Int

Integers are how you will store numbers for the most part. Because most Arduinos have a 16-bit system, the minimum value is -32,768 and maximum value of an integer is 32,767. The Arduino Due and a few other boards work on a 32-bit system, and thus can carry integers ranging from -2,147,483,648 to 2,147,483,647. Remember these numbers when you are attempting arithmetic with your program, as any numbers higher or lower than these values will cause errors in your code.

Unsigned Int

An unsigned integer frees up the 16th bit in the 16-bit system since the first bit is no longer being used as a positive or negative sign. This yields the ability to store numbers from 0 to 65,535 on the 8-bit boards with which you will likely be working. If you have higher values than the signed integers will allow, you can switch to unsigned integers and achieve the same amount of range but all in the positive realm, such that you have a higher absolute value of range.

Word

A word stores a 16-bit unsigned number on the Uno and on other boards with which you will likely be working. In using the Due and the Zero, you will be storing 32-bit numbers using words. Word is essentially the means by which integers and numbers are stored.

Long

If you need to store longer numbers, you can access 4-byte storage, or 32-bit storage in other words, using the long variable. You simply follow an integer in your coded math with the capital letter *L*. This will achieve numbers from -2,147,483,648 to 2,147,483,647.

Unsigned Long

The way to achieve the largest numbers possible and store the largest integers possible is to direct the microcontroller using the unsigned long variables. This also gives you 32 bits or 4 bytes to work with, but being unsigned, the 32nd bit is freed from indicating the positive or negative sign in order to give you access to numbers from 0 to 4,294,967,295.

Short

This is simply another way of indicating a 16-bit datatype. On every type of Arduino, you can use short to indicate you are expecting or using integers from -32,768 to 32,767. This helps free up space on your Due or Zero by not wasting space on 0's for a small number and by halving the number of bits used to store that number.

Float

A float number is a single digit followed by 6 to 7 decimal places, multiplied by 10 to a power up to 38. This can be used to store more precise numbers or just larger numbers. Float numbers take a lot more processing power to calculate and work with, and they only have 6 to 7 decimals of precision, so they are not useful in all cases. Many programmers actually try to convert as much float math to integer math as possible to speed up the processing. In addition, these take 32 bits to store versus the normal 16 bits, so if you're running low on storage, try converting your float numbers to integers.

Double

This is only truly relevant to the Due, in which doubling allows for double the precision of a float number. For all other Arduino boards, the floating point number always takes up 32 bits, so floating does nothing to increase precision or accuracy.

Functions

DIGITAL I/O

pinMode()

This is the notation you will use to set a pin's mode, whether it be INPUT, OUTPUT, or INPUT_PULLUP. The syntax you will use is:

pinMode(pin#, mode)

such that setting analog pin 5 to INPUT would look like this:

pinMode(A5, INPUT)

digitalWrite()

This will write a HIGH or LOW value to a digital pin. You will write:

digitalWrite(HIGH)

OR

digitalWrite(LOW).

This will tell the pin whether to allow the maximum voltage through and into the connected LED or device, or to shut off and not let any current through, essentially turning the device or LED off.

digitalRead()

This is a way to read the data that is measured by a certain or specific pin. It reads HIGH or LOW. The syntax used is:

digitalRead(pin#)

such that if you want to read the measurements from pin 3, you would write the code:

digitalRead(3).

ANALOG I/O

analogRead()

This will read the information being fed into the specific analog pin that you choose and map out the results versus time, with integer values between 0 and 1023. This is a 10-bit analog to digital converter, and hence the numbers you can read will be between the minimum of 0 and the maximum of 1023. It can read as many as 10,000 times per second.

The syntax for this is as you might expect, such that reading analog pin A4, you would write:

analogRead(A4)

analogWrite() – PWM

This will use one of the PWM pins, since the analog pins are specifically for input. It can use the information from an *analogRead* function to create a response. For example, it can change the speed of a motor or brightness of an LED. The values of the *analogWrite* function are between 0 and 255, so to get an allowable number from the 0 to 1023 *analogRead* function, you will need to divide by 4, to make the range between 0 and 255.

Here is an example:

```
void loop()
{
  val = analogRead(analogPin);
  analogWrite(ledPin, val / 4);
}
```

This code will allow you to see in the brightness of the LED how quickly a wheel is turning or some other varying input value.

Chapter 6: Some Other Projects You Can Work On with Arduino

While working on the basic projects in the previous chapter, you should have gotten a basic feel for how the the Arduino programming language works. This should make it a bit easier to move onto other projects that require some trickier code. For most projects, you will be able to simply connect a few supplies, type in the right code, and you will be all set.

This chapter is going to take some time to look at a few more projects that you may want to give a try. While they have longer codes than before and may seem complicated in the beginning, they really aren't too complicated once you grow more familiar with using Arduino.

Here are some cool projects for you to try out for yourself!

LED strip light up

The first project we are going to work on is fun and simple, and will deal with e-textiles. We are going to work on a simple LilyPad Arduino LED Light-up. The tools that you will need to make this are:

- A rainbow LED strip
- Scissors
- Coin cell battery
- Needles
- A LilyPad coin cell battery holder
- Conducting thread bobbin
- Needle threader
- Fabric

- Embroidery hoop

To get started, you will need to thread the needle with the conductive thread. You can then use the embroidery hoop to set the fabric until it becomes taut. Make a positive trace, which is a mark that leads from the power supply over to the positive side of the LED strip. This particular trace is going to start from the battery pack. You can place the battery pack, leaving the battery out, near where the LED will be placed, but make sure that one hole with a plus and one with a negative are pointed towards the location of the LED. These are going to be the negative and positive pins of the battery pack.

Once you have the battery back in the right place, you can start the sewing process. Trap the edge of the board with the fabric by wrapping it in the thread about three times on each of the positive pins on the board. When you are sewing these pins, you do not do it in just one big stitch; it should be done with smaller stitches so that it will stay nice and tight, and won't move around and have the circuits short out.

You should continue to stitch with this thread all through the positive side of your LED strip, sewing it down like the other positive pins. Check to make sure that you have the right pole, because the LED is not going to light up if you connect up the opposite poles.

Now it is time to work on the negative trace. This is going to return from the current part of the LED strip to the negative side of the pack. You will need to follow the same instructions as before, but now you are going in the opposite direction.

When you are done sewing, you need to make sure that the thread doesn't have any parts that are dangling and that the negative and positive traces are not touching any of the parts.

The next step once everything is sewed together is to put the battery into the pack. The LED should already be set up to light right away, and just like that you've powered a light up LED strip with your Arduino!

Heated Blanket

This project is going to be to create a heated blanket using Arduino. It is a little more complicated than the previous project, but is still suitable for beginners. The tools that you will need for this are:

- Red hook up wire

- LilyPad Arduino board

- A wall adapter for power supply (5V DC 1A)

- N-Channel MOSFET 60V 30A

- 2 5X15 Heating pads

- Switch

- Conductive thread

- LIlyPad LED light

- Black hook up water

The first thing that you will need to do is sew up the hand warmer blankets. Get creative here and sew it to look however you desire.

Next, you will need to follow the sewing pattern that we did on the previous project, using the conducting thread to sew onto the board and then connect its edges to the positive side where the LED lights that are blue are located. The negative parts will need to be sewn and connected together as well.

Now, take the hook up wire that is red and connect the positive contact of the board with the positive side of the switch. You can use the parallel connection to connect it at the same time to the positive part of the heating pad. Check to see that you are soldering the connection rather than using the conductive thread.

Getting the negative part to connect is a bit harder. You will need to use the hook up wire that is black to connect your negative parts of the board to the negative parts of the power source. This will then be connected to the negative part of the switch.

You can now create a parallel connection that goes to the S leg of the MOSFET.

You can then create another parallel connection so that it goes to the 10K resistor.

Now it is time to hook up the 11th pin in the board to the G leg of the MOSFET, with a branch that goes parallel to the other end of your resistor.

Connect the D leg of this MOSFET to the negative contacts on the heating blanket.

At this point, it is time to use the IDE for your Arduino to work on writing some code. The code that you will need to write out to make this work is:

```
language:C
/*
Hardware Connections:
-led1 = D9;
-led2 = D10;
-led3 = D11;
-button = D2;
-Mofset = D3;
*/
int btnPin = 2;
boolean btnPressed = false;
```

```
int fetPin = 3;

int led1 = 9;

int led2 = 10;

int led3 = 11;

int mode;

void setup(){

// initialize the digital pin as an output.

pinMode(btnPin, INPUT);

pinMode(fetPin, OUTPUT);

pnMode(led1, OUTPUT);

pinMode(led2, OUTPUT);

pinMode(led3, OUTPUT);

}

// the loop routine runs over and over again forever:

 void loop(){

// increment mode on depress, unless mode = 3, then reset to 0

if (btnPressed && digitalRead(btnPin) == LOW)

mode = mode == 3 ? 0 : mode + 1:

// Assign button state

btnPressed = digitalRead(btnPin):

switch (mode)

{

        case 0:

        analogWrite(fetPin, 0); // off
```

```
digitalWrite(led1, LOW)
digitalWrite(led2, LOW)
digitalWrite(led3, LOW)
break;
case 1:
analogWrite(fetPin, 85); // 33% duty cycle
digitalWrite(led1, HIGH);
digitalWrite(led2, LOW);
digitalWrite(led3, LOW);
break;
case 2:
analogWrite(fetPin, 170); // 66% duty cycle
digitalWrite(led1, HIGH);
digitalWrite(led2, HIGH);
digitalWrite(led3, LOW);
break:
case 3:
analogWrite(fetPin, 255); // 100% duty cycle
digitalWrite(led1, HIGH);
digitalWrite(led2, HIGH):
digitalWrite(led3, HIGH);
break;
    }
}
```

This may look like a really long string of code when you are first getting started, but it is going to give the directions that you need to the heating blanket. Not only is it telling the blanket how to turn on and off, but it is making it possible to pick from a few different heat levels. You will be able to go with a light heat, medium heat, medium hot heat, and a hot heat.

LCD RGB Shaded Glasses

For this project, you will need:

PCB

68 X WS2812 LEDs

68 X 100nF 0805 Capacitors

An Arduino microcontroller, preferably a smaller model

3 pin male header

External power source (ie: a power bank)

Cables to connect the Shades to the power source and to the Arduino

Instructions

1. The first thing you might want to do is test all of the LEDs, since they will be running serially, one bad LED will ruin the entire line of current and cause the entire thing to malfunction or not function at all.

2. Now, solder the capacitors in place and the LED's overtop. You might break LEDs in the process, so be sure to pick up a few spare while you're out purchasing them.

3. Next, connect the port called S on the Shades to the 3rd pin, Pin 3, on your Arduino. GND must then be connected to GND of the external power supply and to

the GND of the Arduino, using the 3 pin male header. Finally, in this step, connect the VCC to the +5V external power supply. MAKE SURE YOU DO NOT EXCEED THE VOLTAGE indicated by the Arduino, or you will destroy the circuitry.

4. You will now use the code below, playing with it to make it your own, in order to create a color distribution that you like. Make sure to read the comments in the code, marked at the beginning of a single line comment by // and a multi-line comment starting with /* and ending with */.

CODE

```
#include "FastLED.h"

// How many leds in your strip?
#define NUM_LEDS 68

byte pixelType = 0;
byte drawIn[4];
byte frameIn[NUM_LEDS*3];


// For led chips like Neopixels, which have a data line, ground,
and power, you just
// need to define DATA_PIN.  For led chipsets that are SPI
based (four wires - data, clock,
// ground, and power), like the LPD8806 define both
DATA_PIN and CLOCK_PIN
#define DATA_PIN 3
//#define CLOCK_PIN 13

// The bluetooth module pins
#define RX_PIN 0
#define TX_PIN 1

// Define the array of leds
```

```
CRGB leds[NUM_LEDS];

void setup() {
  // Uncomment/edit one of the following lines for your leds
  arrangement.
  // FastLED.addLeds<TM1803, DATA_PIN, RGB>(leds,
  NUM_LEDS);
  // FastLED.addLeds<TM1804, DATA_PIN, RGB>(leds,
  NUM_LEDS);
  // FastLED.addLeds<TM1809, DATA_PIN, RGB>(leds,
  NUM_LEDS);
  // FastLED.addLeds<WS2811, DATA_PIN, RGB>(leds,
  NUM_LEDS);
  // FastLED.addLeds<WS2812, DATA_PIN, RGB>(leds,
  NUM_LEDS);
  FastLED.addLeds<WS2812B, DATA_PIN, GRB>(leds,
  NUM_LEDS);
  // FastLED.addLeds<NEOPIXEL, DATA_PIN>(leds,
  NUM_LEDS);
  // FastLED.addLeds<APA104, DATA_PIN, RGB>(leds,
  NUM_LEDS);
  // FastLED.addLeds<UCS1903, DATA_PIN, RGB>(leds,
  NUM_LEDS);
  // FastLED.addLeds<UCS1903B, DATA_PIN, RGB>(leds,
  NUM_LEDS);
  // FastLED.addLeds<GW6205, DATA_PIN, RGB>(leds,
  NUM_LEDS);
  // FastLED.addLeds<GW6205_400, DATA_PIN, RGB>(leds,
  NUM_LEDS);

  // FastLED.addLeds<WS2801, RGB>(leds, NUM_LEDS);
  // FastLED.addLeds<SM16716, RGB>(leds, NUM_LEDS);
  // FastLED.addLeds<LPD8806, RGB>(leds, NUM_LEDS);
  // FastLED.addLeds<P9813, RGB>(leds, NUM_LEDS);
  // FastLED.addLeds<APA102, RGB>(leds, NUM_LEDS);
  // FastLED.addLeds<DOTSTAR, RGB>(leds, NUM_LEDS);

  // FastLED.addLeds<WS2801, DATA_PIN, CLOCK_PIN,
  RGB>(leds, NUM_LEDS);
```

```cpp
  // FastLED.addLeds<SM16716, DATA_PIN, CLOCK_PIN,
RGB>(leds, NUM_LEDS);
  // FastLED.addLeds<LPD8806, DATA_PIN, CLOCK_PIN,
RGB>(leds, NUM_LEDS);
  // FastLED.addLeds<P9813, DATA_PIN, CLOCK_PIN,
RGB>(leds, NUM_LEDS);
  // FastLED.addLeds<APA102, DATA_PIN, CLOCK_PIN,
RGB>(leds, NUM_LEDS);
  // FastLED.addLeds<DOTSTAR, DATA_PIN, CLOCK_PIN,
RGB>(leds, NUM_LEDS);
  Serial.begin(9600);

  pinMode(TX_PIN, OUTPUT);
  pinMode(RX_PIN, INPUT);
}

void loop() {

}

void serialEvent() {
  pixelType = Serial.read();

  switch (pixelType) {
   case 0:
   //draw mode
     while (!Serial.available()) {}
     Serial.readBytes(drawIn, 4);

     leds[drawIn[0]] = CRGB(drawIn[1], drawIn[2], drawIn[3]);

     FastLED.show();
     Serial.flush();
     break;

   case 1:
     //clear mode
     for (int i = 0; i < NUM_LEDS; i++)
     {
       leds[i] = CRGB::Black;
```

```
        }
    FastLED.show();
    Serial.flush();
    break;

  case 2:
    //frame in mode
      while (!Serial.available()) {}
      Serial.readBytes(frameIn, (NUM_LEDS * 3));
      for (int i = 0; i < NUM_LEDS; i++)
      {
        leds[i] = CRGB(frameIn[i * 3], frameIn[(i * 3) + 1],
frameIn[(i * 3) + 2]);
      }

    FastLED.show();
    Serial.flush();
    break;

  case 3:
      while (!Serial.available()) {}
      int brightnessLED = Serial.read();
      FastLED.setBrightness(brightnessLED);
      Serial.flush();

    break;
    }
}
```

5.   Once you have the code to your liking, you can create
     the Arduino sketch file, or .ino file, and upload it to your
     Arduino microcontroller board. Then it's just a matter of
     plugging it into the power source and you will have you
     LED RGB Shades working!

Smart Doorbell

Many times, we find that we miss someone when they stop by, whether because we are not home or even because we do not hear them knock on the door. Here is a solution that will tell you when someone rings your doorbell, notifying you by smartphone message through the application, Blynk, which works on both Android and iOS, and by email if you desire.

The materials you will need for this project include:

An Arduino Uno

Breakout board

Jumper wires

Push button doorbell

Ethernet shield

Blynk application

Instructions

1. First connect the push button to the breakout board.

2. Then connect the ethernet shield to the board so that the push button is connected to network capability.

3. Next, upload the following sketch, inserting your own messages and email address into the code that follows:

```
#define BLYNK_PRINT Serial
#include <SPI.h>
#include <Ethernet.h>
#include <BlynkSimpleEthernet.h>
#include <SimpleTimer.h>

// You should get Auth Token in the Blynk App.
// Go to the Project Settings (nut icon).
char auth[] = "YourAuthToken";
```

```
SimpleTimer timer;

WidgetLCD lcd(V1);

void setup()
{
  Serial.begin(9600);
  Blynk.begin(auth);

  while (Blynk.connect() == false) {
    // Wait until connected
  }
}
void notifyOnButtonPress()
{
  // Invert state, since button is "Active LOW"
  int isButtonPressed = !digitalRead(2);
  if (isButtonPressed) {
    BLYNK_LOG("Button is pressed.");

    Blynk.notify("Please open up! Somebody is on the door!");
    lcd.clear(); //Use it to clear the LCD Widget
  lcd.print(4, 0, "Open"); // use: (position X: 0-15, position Y: 0-
1, "Message you want to print")
    lcd.print(4, 1, "The Door!");
  }
}

void emailOnButtonPress()
{

  int isButtonPressed = !digitalRead(2); // Invert state, since
button is "Active LOW"

  if (isButtonPressed) // You can write any condition to trigger e-
mail sending
  {
    BLYNK_LOG("Button is pressed."); // This can be seen in the
Serial Monitor
```

```
    Blynk.email("youremail@address.com", "Subject: Doorbell",
"Please open up! Somebody is on the door!");
    lcd.clear(); //Use it to clear the LCD Widget
  lcd.print(4, 0, "Open"); // use: (position X: 0-15, position Y: 0-
1, "Message you want to print")
  lcd.print(4, 1, "The Door!");


  }
}

void loop() {
  // put your main code here, to run repeatedly:
  Blynk.run();
  timer.run();
}
```

4.   Finally, connect the Arduino board to the breakout board such that the push button is connected to the input pin and the output pin is connected to the power line.

Those are a few sample projects to get you started with the Arduino!
There are however, plenty more out there available for free that you can try.

Here are a few of the best websites for finding popular Arduino projects for free:

-     https://www.hackster.io/arduino/projects

-     http://www.electroschematics.com/arduino/

-     http://www.electronicshub.org/arduino-project-ideas/

Conclusion

Thanks again for taking the time to read this book!

You should now have a good understanding of how to use your Arduino and be ready to try a few projects!

If you enjoyed this book, please take the time to leave me a review on Amazon. I appreciate your honest feedback, and it really helps me to continue producing high quality books.

www.ingramcontent.com/pod-product-compliance
Lightning Source LLC
LaVergne TN
LVHW050148060326
832904LV00003B/66